Little Books of Guidance

Finding answers to life's big questi...

Also in the series:

THE WAY
OF LOVE

Worship

A little
book of
guidance

CHURCH
PUBLISHING
INCORPORATED

This book compiles text from the following sources:
Christopher L. Webber, *Welcome to Sunday* (Harrisburg, PA: Morehouse Publishing, 2002); Vicki K. Black, *Welcome to the Book of Common Prayer* (Harrisburg, PA: Morehouse Publishing, 2005); Jeffrey Lee and Dent Davidson, *Gathered for God* (New York: Church Publishing Incorporated, 2018); James Farwell, *The Liturgy Explained* (Harrisburg, PA: Morehouse Publishing, 2013); Clayton L. Morris, *Holy Hospitality* (New York: Church Publishing Incorporated, 2005); John Westerhoff, *Living Faithfully as a Prayer Book People* (Harrisburg, PA: Morehouse Publishing, 2004).

Church Publishing
19 East 34th Street
New York, NY 10016
www.churchpublishing.org

Cover design by Jennifer Kopec, 2Pug Design
Typeset by Denise Hoff

A record of this book is available from the Library of Congress.

ISBN-13: 978-1-64065-174-6 (pbk.)
ISBN-13: 978-1-64065-175-3 (ebook)

Contents

Introduction

I pray that you, being rooted and established in love, may have power, together with all the Lord's holy people, to grasp how wide and long and high and deep is the love of Christ, and to know this love that surpasses knowledge—that you may be filled to the measure of all the fullness of God.

—*Ephesians 3:17-19, NIV*

At the 79th General Convention of the Episcopal Church in July 2018, Presiding Bishop Michael B. Curry called the Church to practice *The Way of Love.* This is an invitation to all of us, young and old alike, to "grow more deeply with Jesus Christ at the center of our lives, so we can bear witness to his way of love in and for the world."

With this call, Bishop Curry named seven practices that can help us grow deeper in our relationship with God, Jesus, and our neighbors as we also learn how to live into our baptismal promises more fully. In today's world of busy schedules, hurried meals, and twenty-four-hour news cycles, it is now more imperative that we make and take the time to center ourselves and follow the way of Jesus. This might mean revisioning and reshaping the pattern and rhythm of our daily life—finding a slice of time to center our thoughts on Jesus. Within these pages you will find ideas to engage in the practice of worship as you walk on *The Way of Love: Practices for a Jesus-Centered Life.*

To be a Christian is to be a seeker. We seek love: to know God's love, to love, and to be loved by others. It also means learning to love ourselves as a child of God. We seek freedom from the many forces that pull us from living as God created us to be: sin, fear, oppression, and division. God desires us to be dignified, whole, and free. We also seek abundant life. This is a life that is overflowing with joy, peace, generosity, and delight. It is a life where there is enough for all because we share with abandon. We seek a life of meaning, giving back to God and living for others and not just for ourselves. Ultimately we seek Jesus. Jesus is the way of love and that has the power to change lives and change the world.

How are we called to practice the Way of Love? Bishop Curry has named seven practices to follow. Like a "Rule of Life" practiced by Christians for almost two thousand years, these are ways that help us live intentionally in our daily life, following our deepest values. These are not add-ons to our day, but ways to recognize God working in us and through us.

When we worship, we gather with others before God. We hear the Good News of Jesus Christ, give thanks, confess, and offer the brokenness of the world to God. As we break bread, our eyes are opened to the presence of Christ. By the power of the Holy Spirit, we are made one body, the body of Christ sent to live the Way of Love. After Jesus' crucifixion, his friends' eyes were opened and they recognized him as the Risen Christ when they broke bread and blessed it together. By gathering in community weekly to thank, praise, and dwell with God we, with God's help, "continue in the apostles' teaching, fellowship, in the breaking of bread, and in the prayers."

Practices are challenging and can be difficult to sustain. Even though we might practice "solo" (e.g., prayer), each practice belongs to the community as a whole in which you inhabit as a whole—your family, church, or group of friends. Join with some trustworthy companions with whom to grow into this way of life; sharing and accountability help keep us grounded and steady in our practices.

This series of seven Little Books of Guidance are designed for you to discover how following certain practices can help you follow Jesus more fully in your daily life. You may already keep a spiritual discipline of praying at meals or before bed, regularly reading from the Bible, or engaging in acts of kindness toward others. If so, build upon what we offer here; if not, we offer a way to begin. Select one of the practices that interests you or that is especially important for you at this time. Watch for signs in your daily life pointing you toward a particular practice. Listen for a call from God telling you how to move closer. Anywhere is a good place to start. This is your invitation to commit to the practices of **Turn—Learn—Pray—Worship—Bless—Go—Rest**. There is no rush, each day is a new beginning. Follow Bishop Curry's call to grow in faith "following the loving, liberating, life-giving way of Jesus. His way has the power to change each of our lives and to change this world."

1 ▪ What Is Worship?

Some people come into an Episcopal church for the first time and are thrilled with the worship they discover; others come in and are baffled. No matter what their point of view, newcomers often find themselves in the same boat as the old Scots sea captain who wandered into an Episcopal church one Sunday. Although he was unfamiliar with the service, he later told friends he had survived by "putting down my anchor and rising and falling with the tide." Like the sea captain, there are many worshipers at the Episcopal Church, some of them longtime members, who are still somewhat mystified by the service they take part in every week. They have never really begun the journey to unlock its full richness and meaning. A successful sea captain understands the stars and tides, and plans a trip to take advantage of them. And it is always better to understand the details, too, so our spiritual journey will have greater direction and depth. By learning more about worship—and most particularly worship within the Episcopal Church and the Anglican Communion, you will participate with new understanding, and be enriched by the experience.

The last book of the Bible, the Book of Revelation, portrays heaven itself as one great outpouring of worship. An old Scottish catechism, which the sea captain might have memorized, says that the chief end of human life is "to worship God and enjoy him for ever." If that is true, and we were, indeed, made for worship and are intended to offer worship eternally, it makes good sense to invest time and thought in learning to do it better now.

But what do we mean by worship? Many church notice boards speak of "Worship Services" but what happens at the advertised hour may be different in every parish. At some churches, "worship" consists of hearing a sermon, singing hymns, listening to prayers, and putting money in the collection plate; at others it is an outpouring of gospel hymns and speaking in tongues; at still others, it means watching a priest at a distant altar. For worshippers themselves, the experience varies as well: it may be primarily intellectual, or emotional, or mostly a matter of habit. Whatever worship looks like or feels like, it is only a means to an end: to create and nourish a relationship with God with other Christians. Worship has to do with relationships, and Christians believe that life itself is a matter of relationships: we are who we are because of the people to whom we are related. If we are related to no one, we die. If we are related to God, we live. Therefore we worship.

Human relationships vary widely: some vital and emotional, some are primarily intellectual, some casual and occasional. A few special ones remain a constant part of our lives. Our relationships with God can fit into all those categories also. As a relationship between husband and wife would be unsatisfactory if it were simply intellectual or purely emotional, so a relationship with God is unsatisfactory if it is incomplete. Any relationship is certainly better than nothing, but growth in our relationship with God is essential to our spiritual life. St. Augustine is often quoted as having said, "You have made us for yourself, O Lord, and our hearts are restless until they find rest in you." Worship, in other words, is not an optional relationship but one vital to our health and well-being. We were made for worship. Without it, we are likely to be plagued by the nagging feeling that something is missing from our lives. Yet how many of us put worship at the center of our lives or make any significant effort to grow in our understanding of worship? We aren't likely to focus on it unless we know at the center of our being how much our lives depend on worship, how much they are enriched by it.

Let's admit right away that thinking about worship as a matter of relationships is not always comfortable for Americans. We hear people say, "I have my own religion" or "I can worship God in my own way." If that were true, and worship were primarily a solitary pursuit, it would be fundamentally different from almost every other aspect of human life. Human beings can't live alone. Primitive people knew that: they had to work together to ensure the tribe's survival. Scholars tell us that the Hebrew language of the Bible has no word for an individual body, only for the flesh of which we are all made. It seemed obvious to the Hebrews that life is shared, that our whole existence is bound up with others. But somehow we like to imagine that we can "get along" by ourselves, as if the complexities of modern society had reduced our need for each other. The fact is, modern technology has made us more dependent on each other than ever, and at the same time has created a rising tide of dissatisfaction. Although we are linked with each other more closely than ever by jet planes and e-mail, many people feel alienated, that their lives are incomplete and unsatisfying. Some imagine that the solution is to find ways to drop out or get away from it all. What we need instead is to offer our lives to God in worship so that the pressures and tensions are transformed. The "global village" we have discovered needs a soul.

Christians speak of being part of the "Body of Christ"; St. Paul says we are "members of Christ" as truly as hands and feet and head are part of a body and depend on each other. Coming together for worship, then, is a very natural way of acting out the connection that is already deeply part of our humanity. We are "members one of another," sharing a common life and uniting in common worship. The book Episcopalians use is called a "Book of Common Prayer" for good reason.

Worship may be intended to prepare us for heaven, but we need to admit right away that worship in the Episcopal Church is not always heaven on earth. It can be wrinkled and torn by human foibles and idiosyncrasies. Perhaps the preacher has an odd habit of addressing his remarks to a spot somewhere in the rafters, or one of the acolytes is constantly fiddling with the rope around her vestment, or the organist's hymnal falls on the keyboard shattering a solemn moment, or someone in a nearby pew whispers loudly to a friend during silent prayer. In a baseball game, the errors are recorded for all to see on the scoreboard, but in most human activities, we accept them as part of the human package. In spite of the distractions that are part of life, most of us know how to get our job done and still attend to those we love. So, too, in worship we express our love for God and realize God's love for us in an imperfect world, but we will do it better and with less concern for the interruptions as we grow in understanding and experience. Worship, like anything worthwhile, rewards the effort we make. The great saints of the past and faithful Christians we know can assure us that a deeper relationship with God is well worth the time spent in church.

Is it really possible, then, to have "our own religion" or our own way of worship? Is there nothing to be learned from the great saints of the past or the more experienced Christians around us? A recent article about children and computers reported that boys tend to ignore instructions and "just punch buttons until something works." Maybe that's what some of us do when it comes to worship. But computers are only toys we create for our use; God, on the other hand, created us and remains beyond the comprehension of the greatest scholars or most deeply committed saints. There is always more to learn, more growth that's possible.

Episcopalians often point to the use of standing, kneeling, sitting, communal eating and drinking, the occasional uses of incense and fragrant oils as the physical, material foundation of our worship. Perhaps, we think, if we express our faith on Sunday in material ways and use material things as an expression of our faith, we will be able to connect our faith with the rest of our lives more easily. Two words sum up this point of view: one is "incarnation" and the other is "sacrament." Both are central to an understanding of the way Episcopalians worship.

Christian faith begins with the incarnation: the Son of God coming into the world in human flesh and blood. "The Word became flesh," says St. John's gospel, "and lived among us" (1:14). God did not send us merely good ideas or spiritual notions; God became flesh, outwardly visible to us so that the gospel proclaims not only "what we have heard, what we have seen with our eyes," but also "what we have . . . touched with our hands." Only when God came to us in human flesh could flesh and blood human beings fully understand who God is. For Anglicans, the incarnation has always been central. It is no coincidence that Christmas, the celebration of the incarnation, brings with it so many English customs. In Puritan New England, celebrating Christmas was illegal; but Anglicans continued to deck the hall with boughs of holly, stir up the plum pudding, and remember the poor in doing so. In Charles Dickens' famous story, "A Christmas Carol," when Scrooge finally catches the spirit of Christmas, he sends a plump goose to his poorly paid clerk. Faith in an incarnate Savior needs to be expressed in outward and visible ways.

A faith centered on the incarnation is expressed quite naturally through sacraments. The Prayer Book defines a sacrament as "an outward and visible form of an inward and spiritual grace." Just as God's Word is expressed most fully in Jesus, the Son of God made

5

human, so God speaks to us also through other material means. New members are received into the church through baptism in which water symbolizes our renewal—it's the outward sign of God's grace at work to renew our lives. Week by week we come to the altar to receive the bread and wine through which the life of Christ comes into our lives. The body of Christ is joined with our bodies, and his life-giving blood courses through our veins and arteries. God's love becomes tangible: we can taste it on our tongues. Being human, we need such evidence.

Just as a man and a woman who have fallen in love need to touch each other and hold each other, need to feel physically the invisible love they know, so human beings need outward expressions of their faith. Jesus himself gave the disciples bread and wine as evidence of his presence with them. He also laid his hands on the sick and anointed blind eyes with spittle. The incarnate Savior inevitably used sacramental means to make God's love and healing clear.

So it was natural, from the earliest days of the Church, for Christians to use sacramental expressions of their faith in their worship. When Roman officials in the second century came to arrest the members of a Christian congregation, they made an inventory of the church's possessions, which included candles, plates, cups, vestments, and books. Even under persecution, Christians felt a need to accumulate these materials to enrich their worship. When persecution ended, Christians indulged that impulse openly by building great churches, and embellishing them with mosaic tile and elaborate vestments. Yes, there can be too much of such things—and eventually there were. We can spend so much energy on the outward expression of our faith that we lose all sight of the inward. Rather than go from one extreme to the other, it seems best to balance both aspects of our existence. There is nothing to be gained by denying the reality of the physical world and the bodies that God created and called good. A church that shuns material things denies this basic truth: that the God who created material things used those same things to become known to us. It is fitting and inevitable that such a God be worshiped with and through outward and visible forms.

Recall the story Jesus told of two men who went up to the temple to pray. Both men remained standing, but one told God of his achievements while the other "standing far off, would not even look up to heaven, but was beating his breast and saying, God be merciful to me, a sinner" (Luke 18:9). He expressed penitence not by kneeling, but by the place where he stood, his downcast eyes, and the motion of his arm. Posture and gesture are important means of expression, but what we do, and how we do it, are conditioned largely by our culture, upbringing, and local customs. Our postures and gestures merge into a very slow and stately dance, we use our bodies to express our thoughts and feelings more fully than words can. Every member of the congregation is invited to join in the music and movement of the liturgy to the degree that they are able. We all have a part to play according to our interests and ability. There is no one "right" way or "wrong" way—with the exception of allowing ourselves to become mere spectators.

2 ▪ Why Worship?

The story is told of a young man, an unsavory type, who falls in love with a saintly young woman. Knowing that she will not so much as look in his direction, he slips into the vault of the town cathedral, dons one of the masks of the saints used in the annual town festival, takes on the demeanor and behavior of a saint, and begins to woo her. Surely enough, over time, she begins to fall in love with him. As the relationship flowers and deepens, the young man's scoundrel friends finally become envious of his success with the saintly young woman and, one day, out of sheer spite, challenge him in the center of the town square, in the presence of his beloved, to take off the mask and reveal his true identity. Dejected, knowing that all is lost, he slowly removes the mask . . . only to reveal that his face has become the face of the saint.

The origin of this story is uncertain. Its inspiration, however, is clearly medieval dramas, eighteenth-century stories of the masque, and even St. Augustine's theological account of desire in our search for God.

Whatever its source, it is an apt metaphor for the function of liturgy in the best possible case. *The Liturgy* is the shorthand term we use for the service of worship called, by various families of Christian faith and practice, The Holy Eucharist, the Mass, the Divine Liturgy, Qurbana, Communion, or the Lord's Supper. In due course we will explore the meaning of the liturgy, consider the use of *liturgy* as a term for the Eucharist, and reflect on its structure and the practices. But first, our story.

In the liturgy, the people who call themselves followers of God don a mask, as it were. In the liturgy, they enact in ritualized ways the actions and attitudes befitting those who are followers of the God of Jesus of Nazareth. In the liturgy, they praise the source of beauty and truth, listen to the proclamation of love and the laws of human flourishing in the kingdom of God, lament that which is broken in the world, focus their energy on help for those broken, acknowledge their failings and commit to begin again to seek God and the good, make peace with one another, and welcome one another to a shared table. Like the young man in the story, they seek the one they love, or try to love, or want to love more deeply, and they do so by behaving—again, in "ritual shorthand"—in ways that are congruent with the nature of the One they love. They bring their desires for God and for Life—sometimes focused and afire, though often enough halting, partial, and unfocused—and they direct their actions of worship, praise, lament, and prayer toward the object of their desire, the One from whom all good, mercy, and truth flow out into a broken but glorious creation of which they are a part. Ideally, over time, as they wear that mask of desire for God, ritually enacting peacemaking, welcome, intercession, and sociality, they become like that for which they long. They become more like the persons they aspire to be for the sake of the One they love.

There is deep wisdom to this story. As old as Aristotle's ethics and as new as modern moral and psychological theories is the understanding that we become the persons we want to be by first acting like the persons we want to be, even before we fully feel ourselves to be such persons. Too, the wisdom is there in the mask story that we become like what we desire, and so we do well to take care with our desire and place it, above all, in that which is most deeply worthy of being desired. Being clear about our highest, ultimate desire brings clarity and order to the many other desires we have.

Of course, like all stories and metaphors, the mask story has its limits. Liturgical action, at its best, is indeed like the actions of the young man who seeks to be in a loving relationship with the one he desires and who becomes more like her over time, winning her over in the end. But unlike the young man in the story, in the case of the liturgy, Christians are always already taking the *second* step in an unfolding narrative of love's emergence: it is, as St. Paul and St. John wrote, God who first loves, who IS love, and we whose love is first awakened and focused by the love we have received. Like Michelangelo's painting, God's hand reaches for Adam—for humanity, both women and men—and Adam reaches back, even if haltingly, responding to the divine initiative. Liturgy, as Robert Taft puts it, happens in the gap between the two hands reaching for one another: one in action, one in response.[1]

If the ultimate purpose of liturgy is an action in which human beings "practice" who they are, or desire to be, in response to the One who loves them first, then perhaps we can understand who Christians are meant to be by exploring the meaning of the term *liturgy*, looking at the structure of the liturgy, and reflecting on the practices that make up the structure. That is the purpose of this book: to explain the liturgy and, in the course of doing so, to linger over Christian identity itself.

What we will discover in our study is that being Christian—contrary to an unfortunate, and widespread, misunderstanding—is not really about *holding certain beliefs about God and the world*, but about *becoming a certain kind of person before God and in the world*.

Being Christian turns out to have a great deal to do with being a person who is fundamentally grateful to God for life, committed to living in communion with others, and acting compassionately toward other beings, just as Jesus Christ has done. And liturgy has a great deal to do with becoming Christian.

11

To understand this, and before explaining the liturgy of the Eucharist, we might best begin by reflecting on the term *liturgy* in relation to several other terms to which it is related. After all, if the service of Holy Eucharist is called the *liturgy,* where does this term come from and what does it mean?

Ritual

Let us begin by considering a generic term to which our question is related: that term is ritual. All religious traditions involve rituals. Indeed, ritualizing is something all human beings do, whether they consider themselves "religious" in the narrow sense or not. We relate to the world, convey what we think is most important, and make our way through the passages of life through various rituals. Some rituals are religious (depending on how one defines "religious"); many are civic, or social, or communal. Rituals are seen as a dimension of activities as diverse as American Thanksgiving meals, football games, weddings both within and beyond faith communities, New Year's celebrations, and family gatherings of various kinds. Some rituals are loosely organized, like a Thanksgiving meal in which many of the same people will be involved from year to year; traditional foods are often (though not always) served; some (though not all) of the same family jokes and stories will be told; and the sequence of the day will be fairly predictable, though not rigid, involving, perhaps, elements of gathering and greeting; watching or playing of games; eating the foods associated with the ritual; and so on. Some rituals are more tightly organized and scripted, with specific words and actions, organized in a sequence that is invested with importance so that it does not change. Religious rituals are often of this more highly organized kind.

Our tendency to ritualize may at first be puzzling, or we may be tempted to dismiss the importance of rituals. In part this is because we have been taught since the sixteenth century or so to think of our identities as being centered in the thinking and willing part of ourselves—our souls or our minds. But we have bodies; in fact, we don't just have bodies, we are bodies. We are embodied beings, whether one understands that to mean that we are *souls in bodies* as some of our Greek intellectual ancestors tended to do, or *ensouled bodies* as religious traditions like Judaism tend to do, or *bodies with consciousness* as contemporary neurobiology and neuropsychology do. However we understand ourselves as embodied, our embodiment means that we signal our important values and beliefs, and navigate our most significant life passages, by the whole-body activity of ritual. Thus, rituals involve not simply words and intellectual reflection but ceremony and gesture, movement and song, sound and smell.

Sometimes we use the term "ritual" to mean anything we do on a regular basis, like brushing our teeth in the morning. But rituals are not merely things we do repetitively. We may brush our teeth in roughly the same way every morning, but we could do so differently, so long as our teeth get clean. Brushing our teeth has a utilitarian purpose. Rituals in the full sense of the term are done with a certain amount of repetition because they are scripted, figuratively or literally. They have a normative structure that is considered significant to the values or realities that they are aimed toward, and those values or realities are themselves considered significant in an ultimate way.

Rituals are not simply utilitarian; they don't simply get something accomplished but situate the practitioners within a higher value or set of values that give life meaning. Ritualizing is centered on the beliefs or values that a particular person, group, or culture considers in some way central to their identity and flourishing. It is centered on them in the mode of practice, not simply by way of ideas.

Furthermore, rituals are not simply dramatic expressions of those central things we believe anyway or that happen to us elsewhere. While there are some exceptions, often enough rituals actually enact what we believe, bring to pass certain states of being. Everyone is familiar with a wedding or blessing of a lifelong relationship, and this is a good example of the way in which rituals enact reality. When a couple participates in a marriage or blessing ritual, they are not simply dramatizing a covenantal relationship that has already occurred, though certainly it has begun to take shape in the life of the couple. They are not just announcing something to the public in a particularly festive way. The couple cannot "believe themselves" into being married. Rather, in the course of the ceremony, the marriage itself is actually brought to pass.

When the ritual begins, the couple has a relationship and an intention to make it covenantal and faithful and compassionate, but they are not married, no matter how much they wish or intend to be. Through the marriage rite, they become married; the ritual points to their relationship and their intentions for lifelong commitment, but it also brings to pass that to which it points.

Really, most rituals work in this way, and not just in Christianity, but there is a special term Christians use for rituals that bring to pass what they point to: sacraments. The line between rituals in general and sacraments in particular is not really absolute, but a sacrament is a core ritual and is used to refer to the materiality, the physical objects or signs through which ritualizing enacts identity. Sacramental materials are usually of an elemental nature: food, water, oil, for example. In some religious traditions, such as Hinduism, fire or other natural elements could be said to function sacramentally. In

Christianity, in the ritual of Eucharist that concerns us in this book, the sacramental material is bread and wine. These are foods that, when used in the ritual of the Eucharist—handled, prayed over, and eaten in highly scripted ways—are taken not simply to remind people of Jesus, or even point to the risen Christ who gave his life as divine love for the world, but to make the risen Christ truly present in the lives of those who worship. The bread and wine are not divine; they are not Christ in a literal way; yet they are called the Body and Blood of Christ because in eating bread and drinking wine in this way, the Christ to whom the sacramental foods point is also made really present to the members of the Eucharistic community through the eating of those foods. Christians have had many ways over the years of explaining how the bread and wine convey the real presence of Christ. Here we will content ourselves with the observation that, ritually consumed, they bring to pass that to which they point: the continuing presence of the divine among the human community that desires God and seeks to live, like the young man in our story, in a way befitting the One we love—the One who first loved us.

Christians believe the sacrament of the Eucharist makes God present through Christ in this way we have described, not because the ritual itself contains some special power to do so, but because Jesus told his disciples, at the last meal eaten with them before his death, to eat bread and wine in this way in memory of him. The Jewish form of memory from which Jesus worked is one in which the past is not simply recalled but made present. So in the Eucharist, a ritual of thanksgiving to God ("thanksgiving" is roughly what the term Eucharist means), Christians offer praise to God, hear their sacred Scriptures read, make various responses to those scriptural words, and then eat bread and drink wine through which (by God's grace) the Lord of the community is made present to them again.

Eucharist, then, is a sacramental ritual in which something—God's presence through Christ—is not simply recalled as past, or pointed to as important, but enacted, made real in the community.

Liturgy

But we still haven't defined *liturgy*. Why do we call the sacramental food ritual of the Eucharist a liturgy? And how is the presence of Christ in that food ritual related to the way we ourselves become Christian?

Among Christian rituals, the Eucharist (or communion, or the Mass, etc.) has a pride of place. While it has been practiced in a variety of ways in different times and places, we have good evidence that this ritual of the Eucharist became very early the principal way in which Christians marked their gatherings weekly—perhaps even daily, in addition to other prayers—in which they understood themselves to be connected again to their Lord, who was risen and ascended but still present to them and empowering them to go out to others with the good news of God's radical forgiveness and unconditional love for the world. Over time, the term *liturgy* came to be used as shorthand for this food ritual. When the term is used broadly, it can refer to any number of rituals that Christians do: burials, daily prayer, ministry to the sick, and so forth. All these liturgies, or rituals, bring to pass the connection to God and related features of Christian identity that they point to. But when the reference is to THE liturgy, in most contexts the reference is specifically to the Eucharist. Why?

In the world in which Christianity emerged—a Greek-speaking, Roman and later Byzantine political and cultural environment—a liturgy (*leitourgia*) was an act done by a benefactor for the sake of the people's common life. It was also closely related to religious rituals performed in the temples that benefactors might support. Two senses of the term, then—a (religious) work *of* the people and a work done *for* the good of the public—came together in Christian usage. That usage suggests the instinct of Christians that in the Eucharist, two things happen: God is thanked and praised, and the church joins in God's own activity to do something on behalf of the world. God, the one true benefactor of the world, has done a work for the world in Jesus Christ, loving it, saving it, and calling it to communion with God. As Robert Taft has put it, in the deepest sense, the one true liturgy is God's work of salvation in Jesus Christ. In the Eucharist, the Christian community joins in that work made present to it again and participates in God's love enacted, made real in the world. The church, in fact, both commits to working together in the great benefaction of God's gift of love through Christ, and is empowered to be part of it. In this way, Christian faith is renewed again and again in the Eucharist, not simply as a set of ideas to be held, but a form of life to be lived.

We can see, then, how the terms ritual, sacrament, and liturgy finally converge on a basic idea for Christians: that through its Eucharistic thanksgiving to God, rendered through the hearing of Scripture and the eating of sacred food, something is not just recalled, but enacted; not just talked about appreciatively but brought to pass again.

We don't just express beliefs in a dramatic way in the Eucharist, but we become, like our young man who acted a certain way until he became who he acted, a people of God who are ourselves a continuing part of what God is doing in the world out of love.

Of course, Christians do not do this perfectly, or immediately, or easily, and there are moments in the liturgy when we acknowledge our own failure to enter fully into participation in the one liturgy of God who is Jesus Christ. We will turn to that element, and all the other elements of the liturgy of the Eucharist soon enough. For the moment, it is worth making sure that we have grasped this central point: that the Eucharist is a ritualization, through the eating of sacred food, of an identity into which we ourselves are called by the grace and invitation of the One who has made us and is the deepest end of our desire.

St. Augustine, a great theologian of the Western church, was once reflecting with the newly baptized on the idea in Christian Scriptures that the church is "the Body of Christ." Augustine pointed to the bread and wine on the altar and said to the newly baptized:

> If it's you that are the body of Christ and its members, it's the mystery meaning you that has been placed on the Lord's table. . . . It is to who you are that you reply Amen, and by so replying you express your assent. . . . So be a member of the body of Christ, in order to make that Amen true. . . . Be what you can see, and receive what you are.[2]

A very similar sentiment is expressed in more contemporary terms by Robert Taft, an Eastern rite Catholic scholar of liturgy. Taft said:

> If the Bible is the Word of God in the words of [human beings], the liturgy is the deeds of God in the actions of those men and women who would live in [God]. . . . The purpose of baptism is to make us cleansing waters and healing and strengthening oil; the purpose of Eucharist is not to change bread and wine, but to change you and me: through baptism and eucharist it is we who are to become Christ for one another, and a sign to the world that is yet

to hear his name. That is what Christian liturgy is all about, because that is what Christianity is all about.[3]

The way in which we enact in liturgy both thanksgiving for the love of God and embodiment of the love of God is through the specific prayers, gestures, words, and actions of the rite. The understanding that we seek of the liturgy is aimed, in the end, not at being informed about the liturgy, but being ready to be formed by it, to embody the love of the One who first loved us.

3 ■ Why a "Book of Common Prayer"?

The Episcopal Church (and before it, the Church of England or Anglican Church), has used a prayer book since its inception. The current, 1979 Book of Common Prayer used by the Episcopal Church has several distinctions. First is its language. Although other Anglican Provinces (other denominations or churches with connections to the Church of England and the Anglican Communion, such as Canada, New Zealand, South Africa, and Australia) have also revised their prayer books in the late twentieth century, the American book was the first revision in non-Elizabethan English. However, while language was the most controversial aspect of this revision, many other significant changes were made. The Eucharist was defined as "the principal act of Christian worship on the Lord's Day," thus replacing Sunday Morning Prayer in many parishes. Common translations of several elements of worship were incorporated into Episcopal liturgies, and a shared lectionary for Sundays and Holy Days was adopted, thus insuring a commonality of worship Sunday by Sunday among liturgical churches.

In addition, in the 1979 prayer book the service of baptism was redesigned to make the public "covenant" nature of our relationship with God clearer and to spell out what it means to be a follower of Christ. Special liturgies for Lent and Holy Week recovered from the practices of the early and medieval church were included, and confirmation was expanded to include an opportunity for the reaffirmation of baptismal vows and for the reception of individuals from other Christian communions.

The Language of the Prayer Book

The question of language is at the very heart of the prayer book: it is a collection of *words*, after all, and the words with which we speak to one another and to God profoundly affect what we believe to be true about ourselves and God. Our praying shapes our believing: the words we use matter. In his volume on the prayer book in the New Church's Teaching Series, Jeffrey Lee notes:

> It is important for worshiping communities to know thoroughly the tradition of their prayer. Not for the sake of liturgical correctness, but for the sake of the gospel. To know the classic shape of a eucharistic prayer is not important because it is an interesting piece of historical detail. It is important because it expresses the relationship of the church to the living mystery of the Triune God.[4]

The words we use to describe God—father, mother, friend, unmoved mover, first principle—both express and shape our theology of who God is and how God relates to the creation. Words have power. We all know the damaging effect a continual barrage of negative words can have on our children (as well as on the adults who speak them). If you have traveled to other countries or attended a lecture or church service offered in a language you do not know, you know how isolating and exclusionary language can be. In an age in which religious language is often used to incite terrorist violence and intolerance of others, we are acutely aware that the words of our prayer can even be a matter of life and death.

Language can be both a window into a deep connection with God and also an impediment to such a relationship. One of the graces of the regular and repeated words of prayer book liturgy is that the words become ingrained in our hearts and minds and no longer need to be "read" but can be prayed in a deeper way that leads beyond words to a connection with God. Like a simple mantra, these fixed and repeated words can open our hearts and minds to deep reverence and love, which is the purpose of Christian worship.

On the other hand, we can also become so attached to the words themselves that we lose sight of the relationship the words were intended to express and encourage. We can become "stuck" in our spiritual lives, praying only with the words and forms that are used in public worship, even in our private devotions. The beautiful words of the prayer book, rather than being windows into God's presence, can become a substitute for a relationship with the living God, keeping God at a safe distance while blocking any real encounter that might change our lives or our understanding of who God is.

In their work of revising prayer books over the centuries, Anglicans throughout the world continue to work through the ways in which language affects individuals and communities. This is a vital though difficult task because, as we noted before, our praying shapes our believing. The words with which we pray both reflect and affect what we believe to be true about God and ourselves.

Attending to the language of our prayer is necessary for keeping our liturgies alive and relevant to the actual lives we live, as well as for ensuring that our common worship is a true and trustworthy source of revelation. To that end, the language of prayer among Christians has changed dramatically over time, especially in the last half century.

Most Episcopal congregations have moved away from the Elizabethan English of the Rite One liturgies of the 1979 prayer book to the contemporary version of American English used in Rite Two. In addition, a number of supplemental prayers and liturgies using "expansive" or "inclusive" language have also appeared in recent years, including inclusive language versions of Rite II Eucharistic Prayers

A, B, and D, authorized for trial use at the 79th General Convention held in Austin in Summer 2018.

Enriching Our Worship 1 and *Enriching Our Worship 2* are two collections of texts authorized by our General Convention for use in parishes. These supplemental prayers and canticles are adapted from other contemporary Anglican prayer books, from Orthodox and medieval western liturgies, and of course from Scripture. These prayers and liturgical texts do seek to address such current concerns as the gendered or hierarchical language we use for God, but they also attempt to return "to the resonant imagery of earlier periods in the Church's history," including often neglected writings of the early church and the medieval mystics.[5]

Supplemental texts such as *Enriching Our Worship* have been at the heart of ongoing revision of the prayer book. The 79th General Convention also acted to encourage worshipping communities "in experimentation and the creation of alternative texts to offer to the wider church," and toward the creation of diocesan liturgical commissions to collect, reflect, teach and share these resources.[6] The priest and liturgist Jennifer Phillips describes the goal of trial use well:

> Ultimately, those liturgical texts that will survive over decades, generations, and occasionally centuries of use are those which touch the hearts and minds of many congregations across differences of place and time, bringing together something universal and something particular, something old and something new. Successful texts are those which are cherished. In times of stress and distress, they contain the phrases which spring to the lips for comfort and strength.

In times of joy, their words leap to mind as fitting praise
for the God who is good beyond all our describing.[7]

We worship according to the prayer book tradition, with its gift
of "ordered freedom," as Lee puts it.[8] This ability to change and adapt
without losing sight of the fundamental, traditional pattern of
Christian worship offers Anglicans tremendous latitude to reform
their liturgies according to the needs and cultural demands of the
time, without disintegrating into a number of individual churches
focused simply on their own self-interests, disconnected from the
wider community.

As prayer books around the world are revised—sometimes quite
radically—to incorporate and reflect the language and culture of the
people who use them, the words of Anglican worship have become
abundantly multicultural and diverse. Yet the pattern of Anglican
worship remains the common ground in which we are rooted. We
may no longer hear exactly the same words spoken when we travel
to other Episcopal and Anglican churches around the world, but we
are still united in the pattern of our common actions. We gather to
be reconciled and to pray for one another, the world, and ourselves.
We gather to be washed in the waters of baptism and to share in the
eucharistic meal that nurtures our common life. We gather to praise
and adore the God who creates, loves, redeems, and sustains all that
is. Whether we read the words undergirding these actions in a well-
worn leather-bound book or follow them in a weekly service bulletin
with texts downloaded from the Internet, we are participating in the
mystery of worship according to the "ordered freedom" the prayer
book tradition both preserves and encourages us to explore.

4 ▪ Living into Our Baptism

The Baptismal Rite represents the most radical reform in the Book of Common Prayer 1979. Among the most significant changes was the moving of the rite for Holy Baptism from the first of the pastoral lifecycle rites to its own special place between the liturgies for the most holy days in the church year and the Holy Eucharist, thereby establishing that Baptism is a full and complete rite of Christian initiation for both children and adult believers rather than a rite of passage related to birth.

Holy Baptism is now to be understood as full initiation by water and the Holy Spirit into Christ's body, the church. The bond that God establishes in Baptism is indissoluble. We can reject and/or distort it, but we can never deny who and whose we are. It is God who is the prior actor in Baptism, an action to which we respond. This explains why a baptism can never be repeated. While we may break our covenant with God, God never breaks God's covenant with us. An appropriate and necessary response to being unfaithful to our baptismal vows and covenant, therefore, is to reaffirm them over and over again.

Baptism makes the baptized person "a" Christian; it tells us the truth about ourselves. But to become Christian, we need to spend the rest of our lives living into our baptism, becoming who we already are. Baptism is intended to be a public act in the presence of a congregation.

From a theological perspective, at Baptism parents give up their children for adoption, adoption into a new family, the church, that accepts them and promises to nurture them in their new life in Christ as well as support their parents and godparents in the keeping of their promises. We do this symbolically by giving each child a baptismal name, such as John Henry or Nancy Caroline, and a new surname, Christian. It is for this reason that in the community's intercessions we do not include the surnames of those who have been baptized, only their Christian names. It is, therefore, most appropriate to celebrate a baptism in the congregation in which the parents and child intend to live and worship, rather than in a grandparent's church or in the church where one of the parents had been baptized. Further, Baptism ought never be a private family event; Baptism is intended to be a church event.

Symbolic Occasions for Baptism

In order to help us better understand Baptism, it is recommended that baptisms be celebrated on five special occasions. The first is the Easter Vigil. Here we are reminded that in Baptism we die to our old self and are reborn with Christ into a new self. This is symbolically made real through immersion (a growing tradition in the Episcopal Church, especially with adults), in which we experience being drowned and resurrected to new life.

A second is All Saints' Day, when we are reminded that in Baptism we are washed clean of all that might separate us from God and made a holy people, that is, saints. Pouring water over the heads of those being baptized is a symbol of this truth.

The next occasion is Pentecost, when we remember that in Baptism we are infused with God's Holy Spirit and thereby empowered to live a new life in faith.

Then there is the Sunday after Epiphany, the baptism of our Lord, which reminds us that Baptism is every Christian's ordination to ministry; to represent Christ and his church; to bear witness to him wherever we may be; and, according to the gifts given us, to carry on Christ's work of reconciliation in the world.

And last is the visitation of the bishop, which reminds us that in Baptism we are incorporated into a new family, the universal family of all the baptized.

Besides water and oil, there are two other historic symbols related to Baptism. First, a baptismal candle is lit from the paschal candle so the person being baptized will remember his or her call to be a light to the world, a sign and witness to the coming reign of God. Second, a cockle shell, a symbol of pilgrimage, holds three drops of water to remind us that we have been baptized into a Trinitarian understanding of God and that we are on a pilgrimage to live into the reality of our baptism.

In Baptism we are incorporated into Christ's body, infused with Christ's character, and empowered to be Christ's reconciling presence in the world.

Regardless of whether we are baptized as children or as adults, sponsors are necessary—the sponsors for children being both the parents and chosen godparents. Sponsors for infants make promises in their name and take vows on their behalf. It is anticipated that parents and godparents will accompany them on their spiritual journey and, by prayer and example, prepare them for their Confirmation, their first public affirmation of their baptismal vows and covenant. It is essential that parents and godparents engage in serious preparation for these rites, for only persons who are on a faithful pilgrimage of living into their own baptism and who take seriously their need to renew their baptismal covenant along the way can faithfully participate in the baptism of an infant they love. This necessary preparation of parents and godparents explains why there is a new rite for the birth or adoption of a child to be celebrated at the Sunday Eucharist shortly after the birth or adoption of a child.

The baptism of an adult or an older child also requires special preparation. Sponsors for adults and older children signify their endorsement of the candidates and their intention to accompany them in their baptismal preparation and to support them by prayers and example in their Christian life. These sponsors are named when an adult or older child ideally begins a year or more of preparation for Baptism. Sponsors for adults or older children assume the same responsibility as sponsors of children and therefore need to be among the most faithful in the parish so that they might perform this important task.

Baptismal Vows

The rite of Holy Baptism begins with the presentation of candidates by their sponsors who have accompanied them during their preparation to receive the sacrament of Baptism. It continues with an acknowledgment that those who are to be baptized seriously desire it. Infants and younger children are presented by their sponsors, parents, and godparents, who promise with God's help to take responsibility for bringing them up in the Christian faith and life. This represents a promise to participate with them in the life of a community of faith and to practice with them the Christian life of faith. It is also a promise to pray with them and for them as well as to be for them an example of the Christian life of faith, thereby assisting this child to live into his or her baptism until she or he is ready to make a mature public affirmation of his or her commitment to the responsibilities of the baptized. There is no more awesome responsibility one can assume, and it ought not to be entered into lightly or without serious preparation.

Immediately thereafter follows a series of vows or declarations in the form of three renunciations and three adherences that are foundational to the life of the baptized and indeed a necessary precondition before persons are able to enter into their baptismal covenant with God faithfully.

A renunciation is an action in which we separate ourselves from a former condition or state by giving up former perceptions and allegiances and accepting the gift of a new set of perceptions and allegiances.

To put it in another way, if you are walking in one direction, you see reality from that perspective and act accordingly. But if you repent, that is, turn around and change the direction you are traveling, you see reality from a new perspective and behave accordingly. That is exactly what a person does when he or she makes these three renunciations and adherences.

Our first act is to renounce evil, that is, to acknowledge evil's influence on our lives and to make a formal declaration to refuse, with God's help, to follow, obey, or be influenced by evil. To renounce evil is also to assert that with God's help we will not permit ourselves to be victimized by our experience of evil—evil that, in this case, is the result of its influence on others whose resulting actions affect us.

To understand the church's understanding of evil is difficult. Despite all attempts to explain it, evil remains a mystery best understood as both an active power or influence that desires to estrange us from God, and the experience of an absence of a God-desired good by the actions of those who have succumbed to evil's influence.

The good news of the Christian faith is that the power of evil to corrupt or destroy us has itself been destroyed. Evil continues to exist; we experience its influence and suffer from its consequences, but it has no power to affect our lives that we do not grant it. It is important to acknowledge that God does not will evil, but evil is a reality of the gift of our human free will, a freedom necessary if we are to experience healthy relationships between ourselves and God, between each other, and between ourselves and the rest of God's creation. These relationships are God's greatest desire and good. Evil would have us misuse or abuse this freedom and thereby disrupt or destroy these relationships.

Sins are actions we engage in that are against God's will, but sin is the disposition to act in ways that negatively affect the relationships God intends for us to have with God, ourselves, other persons, and creation. Sin is not so much concerned with determining what is right or wrong as it is with determining what kind of person we will become if we continue to act in some particular way.

The good news of the Christian faith is that God's redeeming power is ever present, making new life possible. However, if that truth is to operate in us, we in our freedom must renounce the power of evil in our lives.

In the Baptismal Rite, we renounce three distinct manifestations of evil: cosmic evil, systemic evil, and personal evil. The first renunciation is this: "Do you renounce Satan and all the spiritual forces of wickedness that rebel against God?" Cosmic evil would have us believe that we have the power to manage nature and history. We experience cosmic evil in the unmanageability of nature and history. We also experience cosmic evil in physical and mental disease and in natural disasters that cause suffering for those who are not responsible for them. We also experience cosmic evil as a consequence of the actions taken by those who believe they can control nature and history.

The second question concerning renunciation is this: "Do you renounce the evil powers of this world that corrupt and destroy the creatures of God?" Systemic evil would have us believe that we have the power to manage human affairs and the social systems we create. We experience systemic evil as the disordering of human affairs in the structures of society and human relationships. Racism, sexism, classism, nationalism, and militarism are all examples. So are the various social, political, and economic systems we create with good intentions but that result in depriving some person or group of a good that God intends for them.

And the last question concerning renunciation is this: "Do you renounce all sinful desires that draw you from the love of God?" Personal evil would have us believe that we have the power to manage our own lives. We experience the consequences of personal evil when we are influenced by the historic dispositions to sin: pride, envy, nursed anger, sloth, greed, gluttony, and lust, as well as the consequences of our many addictive behaviors, which are themselves expressions of the influence of personal evil.

So it is that we are called upon to acknowledge that our lives are unmanageable and that our desire to be independent, self-sufficient, self-disciplined, self-interested, and self-determined, to be effective, to make a difference, to be successful, to be in control—all values of our secular society that are at the heart of our common human sickness and ultimately the foundation for our destruction—need to be renounced.

In other words, we begin our baptismal vows by admitting that we are powerless over those human dispositions that are a consequence of original sin, a doctrine that acknowledges a contradiction between who we really are as God's creation and how in our freedom we choose to live. Although we are formed in the image of love, the image of God, our souls from the moment of birth are affected by other influences that present us with images for our lives that are less than divine, images of human life that would have us deny and distort our total dependence on God and influence us to desire and act as if we have power that belongs to God alone. Or, in the case of some, to believe that they have no control over their lives at all and are always victims of the past or the actions of others.

Having acknowledged our human condition and renounced evil, we turn to three adherences. Having turned away from and rejected one way of life, we make a faithful attachment of our minds, hearts, and wills to an alternative way of life. That is what we mean by an adherence. Our first adherence is to the affirmation that there is a power greater than ourselves who can help us, namely, Jesus Christ, whom we, therefore, accept as our savior. He is the one who can save us, free us, liberate us from the influence of evil and our disposition to sin. To accept Jesus as our savior, of course, has a consequence that can be frightening. No longer can we blame our heredity or our environment for our human situation or attribute our behavior to the forces of evil in and around us. Now we must take responsibility for our lives. And depending on God to aid us, we can know and do the will of God, that is, live a faithful life. Then, having affirmed Jesus' power to save us, we put our complete trust in his grace and love—we turn our wills and lives over to his care.

At this point in the rite, the congregation composed of recovering sinners—that is, saints who sin, who have witnessed these vows and who know that none of us can make them alone—promises to do all in its power to support those being baptized in their life of faith as members of the body of Christ.

The Baptismal Covenant

Having made these baptismal vows, we are prepared to enter or reenter into our covenant with God. The frame of the creedal dimension of our covenant is "I believe in" and "Amen." The "I" is both personal and communal, in that while each of us must affirm our own faith, the faith we affirm belongs to the community. No one writes his or her own confession of faith; rather, we personally affirm the community's faith, its image of the nature and character of God, and God's promises to us. The "believe in" is not intended to be an intellectual acceptance of propositions concerning doctrinal truth. The phrase is rather an offering of our love, loyalty, devotion, and obedience to a particular image of God. It is an affirmation of faith. While faith can be used to indicate convictions, trust, or worship, faith is best understood as perception, that is, the way in which we see or imagine life and our lives.

Our underlying perception as Christians is that of a triune God: God the Father, God the Son, and God the Holy Spirit. Our God is a God who lives in and for community. To be created in the image and likeness of this God is to have been made for community, a community that comprises great diversity and yet has a common relationship with God. The "Amen" is our public profession that on this faith, this perception of life and our lives, we stake our lives.

By responding to three questions that are answered through a reaffirming of the sacred narrative that is the basis for our life together, we express our faith concerning the nature and character of the God who enters into covenant with us. This God is the one who creates, rules, and orders all life in sovereign, transcendent majesty, and yet who is a loving parent who nurses and nurtures us as sons and daughters. God longs for intimacy with us and for harmonious relations among all creatures and all creation. The world we inhabit belongs to this God, who has a purpose for all of creation and is present and active within it, acting to re-create and redeem all that we do to deny and distort that purpose. And in God's good time, God will, with our cooperation, bring creation and its creatures to their intended end.

This same God, we confess, entered human life and history in the person of Jesus of Nazareth to provide us with an image of who and whose we are and how we are to live. Jesus in his crucifixion joins us in our suffering and, through the power of suffering love, defeats the power of evil. In his resurrection and through the gift of the Holy Spirit, God makes it possible for us to become what God intends us to be: faithful brothers and sisters abiding together as a reconciled and reconciling people in God's reign, that is, a domination-free, nonviolent society of reconciled persons who live by the principle of justice as equity.

This God guides, goads, and strengthens us through the Holy Spirit as we endeavor to know and do God's will. God remains present and active in human life and history as Spirit, especially in the church, through which God is forever offering us reconciliation through the forgiveness of our sins, thereby enabling us to live into the truth of our baptism. This God can be trusted to see that nothing except our own wills can prevent us from fulfilling the meaning and purpose of our lives, that is, to grow into an ever-deepening and loving relationship with God for eternity. And this God is always redeeming our personal and corporate lives, turning negatives into positives, sorrow into joy, illness into health, death into life. Our life with this God of our faith is one of grateful response for all that God has done, is doing, and will do for us. And so we boldly make five promises, aware that God intends to provide us with the help necessary to make good on them.

We first acknowledge the need of life in a community of faith for formation, support, and encouragement; therefore, we promise to live into our baptism through study, personal prayer, and participation in the communal and sacramental life of a congregation.

Next, we acknowledge that while evil has no power over us, its influence surrounds us and without God's help we will surely succumb; therefore, we promise to live self-critical lives that are aware of sin and we commit to changing the direction of our lives continually so as to follow more closely in the way of Jesus.

Third, we acknowledge that we have an obligation to share with others what God has done for us and all people; therefore, we promise to live lives that are a sign and witness, in all that we say and do, to the good news of God's reign, that condition in which God's will is known and done.

We then acknowledge our gratitude for God's unconditional love, which has made a new way of life possible for all humanity; therefore, we promise to help those who reject or distort the truth about themselves to see that there is an alternative way to live by loving them as God has loved us.

And last, we acknowledge that God's reign of justice and peace, that is, of reconciliation, is a reality; therefore, we promise to demonstrate in gestures great and small what it means to live together as a people restored to unity with God and each other in Christ by committing ourselves to honor and respect the uniqueness and value of all people.

Baptismal Renewal and Preparation

There is a difference between being "a" Christian and "being" Christian. When we are baptized we become "a" Christian, but to become Christian takes time and effort. We are always living into our baptism, that is, becoming who we already are. This is accomplished by God's action in our lives to which we respond positively. Therefore, it is expected that we will renew our baptismal covenant over and over again. The first time we do that is known as Confirmation. If a person has been baptized and has already made a public affirmation of faith, regardless of tradition, he or she renews his or her baptismal covenant upon being received into the Episcopal Church. Parents and godparents are reaffirming their baptismal covenant at their child's baptism.

Others may choose to prepare for the reaffirmation of their baptismal covenant at some special transition in their lives, such as those life-cycle years of forty or fifty, before a marriage or after a divorce, upon a move to a new home, a change of parish, or a death. Further, to emphasize the need for renewal, it is expected that everyone in a congregation will renew his or her covenant on the various days set aside for baptisms, even if there is no one to baptize. And remember that Lent is the season for all Christians to prepare to renew their baptismal covenant each year at the Easter Vigil.

A healthy congregation provides the means to help us all to prepare for a meaningful reaffirmation of our baptismal vows and covenant.

Such a process includes two dimensions: formation—an intentional practice of and participation in the Christian life of faith; and education—an intentional process of critical reflection on our lives in the light of the Christian life of faith, that is, on our baptismal vows and covenant.

Christianity is first and foremost a way of life resulting from a particular perception of God and human life that is faith. If we are to live into our baptism, we need to intentionally practice a way of life that includes communal worship, personal prayer, engagement with scripture, being good stewards of all our gifts and graces, practicing acts of love (personal and social) for all others in need, and serving God through our daily lives and work.

To prepare for the renewal of our baptismal vows and covenant, we need to take time to develop a plan for our continuing formation in the Christian life of faith and to reflect on our life experiences and actions as a baptized person. We will also need at least one other person with whom to share our experiences and reflections. Helpful suggestions are provided below, beginning with formational experiences.

Worship: a commitment to increase participation in the celebration of the Eucharist as well as daily morning and evening prayers with at least one other person.

Personal prayer: the development of a more intentional spiritual discipline of silence and solitude, daily devotions, the reading of spiritual classics, and a regular meeting with a spiritual director, confessor, or friend.

Scripture engagement: the establishment of a plan for a more serious reading, study, and meditation on scripture alone or in a group.

Christian service: a more healthy attendance to one's own personal needs and a greater acquaintance with and response to the needs of others, especially the poor, the hungry, the homeless, the sick, and the dying, and a commitment to address their needs by personal acts of caring and social acts of influencing public policy.

Stewardship: the development of a more disciplined life of being more a faithful steward of God's gifts to us and of God's creation.

This would include increasing personal financial contributions to the church and to other needy causes, simplifying your lifestyle, increasing the use of your time and talent in the service of the needy, and engaging in practices that are ecologically sound.

Ministry within daily life and work: this implies being more intentional about understanding your daily life and work as the context for loving and serving God as well as practicing a way of life that manifests this understanding.

Having developed a personal formational program, we need to have at least one other person to help keep us accountable for our plan and with whom we can reflect on our actions and experiences and develop a more faithful life.

The second part of our preparation for the renewal of our baptismal vows and covenant involves critical reflection, a serious consideration of the meaning of these promises, a reflection on how well we have been doing, and specific commitment to be more faithful.

Earlier we discussed a theological understanding of evil. Now is the time to reflect on how we have experienced natural (cosmic) evil, systemic evil, and personal evil in our lives, what it will mean and look like for us to renounce its influence in our lives, and what help we will need from the church if our renunciation is to be sustained.

Then, turning to the adherences in which we commit ourselves to a new way of life, we need to consider what it will cost us to turn to Jesus Christ and accept him as our savior, that is, to acknowledge that we are free to act as healthy, mature persons and we alone are responsible for our thoughts, feelings, and actions. Then consider what it will cost us to rely totally on God's grace and love and finally what it will cost us to follow and obey Jesus. Then, having counted the cost, we need to ask how our new willingness to be faithful in spite of the cost will manifest itself in our lives and determine what help we will need from the church if we are to be faithful to our new resolves.

Having reflected on our baptismal vows, we turn to our baptismal covenant first in terms of the Apostles' Creed, in which we express our love and loyalty to a particular image of God. One way to do that would be to draw one or more pictures to express your experience of the presence or absence of God during the past year. And then reflect on these pictures and complete the following sentences: My relationship to God is like _____. What do I need to do to improve my relationship with God? How can I begin to develop an ever-deepening and loving relationship with God?

Finally, we reflect on each of the promises in terms of the following questions: What have you done about this promise during the past six months? What concretely do you intend to do in the year to come? What will you need from God if you are to realize this promise?

Before you make a reaffirmation of your baptismal vows and covenant before God and the congregation, it may be helpful to go on a short retreat to pray about your preparation and then when you return meet with others who will be renewing their vows and covenant to share and reflect on your experiences. If you are the only one, find a few friends with whom you can share your experience and solicit their help in keeping your new resolves.

5 ■ Worshipping with Thanksgiving

The most common act of worship you are likely to experience in the Episcopal Church is the Holy Eucharist. The word eucharist means "thanksgiving." On any given Sunday in most Episcopal churches, you will find a group of people giving thanks over a simple meal of bread and wine. Christians have done this in some form from the earliest days. In fact, biblical stories that try to convey that Jesus is alive often describe people sharing a meal.

None of this is surprising. Jesus was a real human being.

He learned and laughed and cried and taught and loved and got in trouble with those in power and finally suffered an agonizing death. He ate and drank with all kinds of people, often offending the rigid sensibilities of his day about who was acceptable or not. After his crucifixion, the community of friends and followers that had gathered around him did the same things. They continued to share the meal where Jesus had promised to gather with them.

Back to Emmaus

One of the most precious stories in the Bible is about two friends of Jesus who left Jerusalem on the afternoon of his resurrection, headed to a place called Emmaus (Luke 24:13–35). Were they trying to get out of Dodge? Were they afraid the authorities might come after them next? Were they just trying to escape their grief that Jesus was gone?

We don't know, but Luke tells us that as they walked along swapping stories, a "stranger" comes alongside them, somebody who knows nothing of the stories they share. "Are you the only person who's been in Jerusalem who doesn't know what's happened?" they ask. "What things?" says the stranger. The story turns almost comical here, a little giddy.

They tell him all about Jesus and what has happened, their hopes and dreams about him, the possibility that he was the one to rescue them from the terrible oppression of all that imperial Rome represented, and now all of that is dashed on the cross.

The story goes on. It's getting dark. They come to an inn and beg this stranger to come join them. Suddenly, the table starts to turn. The stranger they've invited to be their guest suddenly becomes their host. He takes the bread, breaks it, and with stunning speed, they get it. Jesus has been walking with them all this way, unrecognized. It wasn't their ideas that revealed him. It wasn't some miracle, nor was it some test they passed. It was the action of breaking open that loaf.

It was the breaking open of their lives.

Those two would never be the same again. The story says they got up and ran back to the one place in all the world they probably thought they would never see again: Jerusalem.

They went back to the scene of their grief and despair, back to the other friends of Jesus with the message that grief and despair isn't all there is. They went back with a word of hope.

They went back with a bewildering experience of joy and a growing conviction that there isn't any hunger God can't fill.

Emmaus is the pattern for what still goes on in church, what happens whenever Christians gather to break bread. In the Holy Land, six miles or so outside Jerusalem, there is a town named Abu Ghosh. It is one of the traditional sites that many Christians through the centuries have identified as the biblical Emmaus. In Abu Ghosh there is a remarkable church building that dates from the Crusader era. Named the Church of the Resurrection, it is now part of a Benedictine monastery.

One of the church's most striking features is its interior walls, which are covered with hauntingly beautiful frescoes, images of biblical scenes, angels and saints. There is a mysterious air about these frescoes because most of the faces have been erased. They were removed when the building was held by Muslim believers, since Islam prohibits any visual portrayals of God or saints.

To gather for the Eucharist in this church today is to be surrounded by the faceless images of ancient, faithful people. Standing there, you have the sense that these people could be anyone, including us. We are, after all, living the pattern they laid out all those centuries ago.

A Container for the Holy

While we can't know precisely what happened in these earliest experiences, we do know these encounters were so powerful that in some sense they launched the whole Christian movement. The first Christians kept the meal that had transformed their lives and allowed it to take a particular shape.

Regular, repeatable gestures, prayers, stories, even the way the food itself is shared—all of that can be described under the heading of ritual. Ritual exists to provide a container for an experience of the holy—something that may have taken your breath away—so that others might encounter it, too.

Ritual is the art of inviting people to be changed.

We call Christian ritual liturgy. The Greek word *leitourgia* meant something like a public work at private expense. In ancient Greece for instance the *leitourgia* referred to public service performed by wealthy citizens for the sake of the common good.

Today in church you will often hear the word liturgy defined as the "work of the people." This definition is usually aimed at reminding worshipers that every member of a worshiping assembly has a part to play, an active role in making the act of worship happen. In the Episcopal Church, as in other liturgical churches, worship is not just about the preacher and whatever edifying thing he or she may have to say. It's not all about the minister. Rather, there are many ministers: readers, musicians, distributers of the bread and wine, ushers, priests, deacons, and more. It takes all of them to make this public offering.

This is why it is increasingly common to hear Episcopalians talk about the priest who is leading an act of worship as the **presider.** The Book of Common Prayer uses the term "celebrant" for this person, but in a real sense, every person who attends the gathering is a celebrant—we are all celebrating this liturgy—or more accurately, it is Christ himself celebrating it in and through his people. We all celebrate; one of us presides.

This dynamic relationship is clear in the dialogue at the opening of the prayer over the bread and wine:

Priest: The Lord be with you.
People: And also with you.
Priest: Lift up your hearts.
People: We lift them to the Lord.
Priest: Let us give thanks to the Lord.
People: It is right to give God thanks and praise.

This dialogue is like a series of questions and answers between priest and people. In effect, the priest is asking the permission of the whole assembly to continue the prayer in its name. When the people say or sing "Amen" (which may be related to a Hebrew word meaning truthfulness) at the end of the whole prayer, they are affirming the truth of what has been prayed. We might translate Amen as "So be it."

This ritual meal takes the whole congregation to make it so.

Making Believe

We are made for ritual. Human beings are symbol-making creatures. If we don't have healthy rituals, we will invent others, good or bad. Think of the highly ritualized behaviors of the professional football game, or the elaborate symbols and initiation rites of sororities and fraternities or the alarming rituals of urban gang culture. Ritual is part of being human.

Christian ritual, the liturgy of the church, is meant to be an invitation to an encounter with the dying and rising Christ, an encounter that can change us and send us to do God's work in the world. While Christians have no exclusive claim on how God chooses to be revealed in this world, we believe that this encounter and this possibility happens reliably, according to the promise of Jesus, in the midst of those who have been made members of Christ's Body through the water of baptism.

The Episcopal way of being Christian is a very practical one. We do not ask people to believe elaborate ideas about God or the Bible or Jesus before they can be counted members. To belong to the Episcopal Church you must simply do what the church does.

The church gathers; that's what the word "church" means.

The word "church" in the Bible comes from the Greek word *ecclesia*, from which we get words like "ecclesiastical." It means "to be called out," as a gathering. And when the church gathers, it gathers for a purpose; it gathers to do something. It's provocative, but you might call our approach to the Christian faith "make believe." Make. Believe.

Make it real. Put it into practice. "Show me." Act like Jesus. Do what he did. Be his hands and heart right now, right here, in this world with its horrors and hungers and heartaches. Start with worship.

6 ▪ The Hospitality of Worship

The Feeding of the Five Thousand

All four gospels tell the story of the miraculous feeding of a huge crowd. Jesus and his friends wanted to get away for a while. They walked into the countryside, and a crowd followed them. As the story goes, five thousand men, with an undisclosed number of women and children, followed Jesus and the disciples, hoping to hear Jesus teach. As the day wore on, it was time for something to eat. There was nothing at hand: no caterer, no fast-food stands. "What do we have?" Jesus asked. "Five loaves and two fish," one of the disciples answered. Jesus took a loaf, broke it, and passed the pieces to people nearby. He made the same gesture with the fish. When the meal was over, baskets of leftovers remained.

What happened? What does it mean?

The simplest exegesis is probably the best. Of course, there were no restaurants in the countryside. But there was lots of food in the city. It would have been almost second nature for folks intending to be in the countryside for the day to grab a little something to take along. One imagines that everyone—at least the adults—would have planned for the inevitability of midday hunger. And so, when Jesus made the initial gesture of hospitality, passing to those nearby the food he had in hand, others reached into their satchels to dig out what they had brought along. It's not hard to imagine why there was so much left over. We humans like to eat. If we're going to err, we're likely to grab too much, not too little.

The feeding of the five thousand is a story about holy hospitality. Jesus does what he always does. He uses the occasion to make a point about the way life is supposed to be. People are to be fed. Life is like a great banquet. Even in the wilderness, with no visible food supply in sight, the crowd is satisfied and there is an abundance of food left over. Alleluia!

The image of abundant food is essential to an understanding of Christian ministry. It's all about feeding and being fed. At any moment in the day, some of us can feed. Some of us need food. The church is about making connections between those who have food and those who need it. The story of the five thousand is a reminder that it isn't all that complicated.

The Baptismal Promises

The 1979 Book of Common Prayer distinguishes itself from its predecessor largely in its insistence on a baptismal ecclesiology. That is, the book assumes that the ministry of the church is carried out in the world by its baptized members. Clergy are set apart to facilitate the ministry of the baptized. They are not set apart to minister on behalf of the congregation, nor are they set apart to provide the members of a congregation with a sense of spiritual wellbeing. This is not to say that clergy have no responsibility for pastoral care, but simply to state as clearly as possible that the church's commitment to service is the work of the people.

Notice these details from the Prayer Book:

From the Catechism ...

The Church

Q. What is the mission of the Church?

A. The mission of the Church is to restore all people to unity with God and each other in Christ.

Q. How does the Church pursue its mission?

A. The Church pursues its mission as it prays and worships, proclaims the Gospel, and promotes justice, peace, and love.

Q. Through whom does the Church carry out its mission?

A. The Church carries out its mission through the ministry of all its members.

The Ministry

Q. Who are the ministers of the Church?

A. The ministers of the Church are lay persons, bishops, priests, and deacons.

Q. What is the ministry of the laity?

A. The ministry of lay persons is to represent Christ and his Church; to bear witness to him wherever they may be; and, according to the gifts given them, to carry on Christ's work of reconciliation in the world; and to take their place in the life, worship, and governance of the Church.

Q. What is the ministry of a bishop?

A. The ministry of a bishop is to represent Christ and his Church, particularly as apostle, chief priest, and pastor of a diocese; to guard the faith, unity, and discipline of the whole Church; to proclaim the Word of God; to act in Christ's name for the reconciliation of the world and the building up of the Church; and to ordain others to continue Christ's ministry.

Q. What is the ministry of a priest or presbyter?

A. The ministry of a priest is to represent Christ and his Church, particularly as pastor to the people; to share with the bishop in the overseeing of the Church; to proclaim

51

the Gospel; to administer the sacraments; and to bless and declare pardon in the name of God.

Q. What is the ministry of a deacon?

A. The ministry of a deacon is to represent Christ and his Church, particularly as a servant of those in need; and to assist bishops and priests in the proclamation of the Gospel and the administration of the sacraments.

Q. What is the duty of all Christians?

A. The duty of all Christians is to follow Christ; to come together week by week for corporate worship; and to work, pray, and give for the spread of the kingdom of God.[9]

From the Baptismal Liturgy . . .

The Presentation and Examination

Q. Do you renounce Satan and all the spiritual forces of wickedness that rebel against God?

A. I renounce them.

Q. Do you renounce the evil powers of this world which corrupt and destroy the creatures of God?

A. I renounce them.

Q. Do you renounce all sinful desires that draw you from the love of God?

A. I renounce them.

Q. Do you turn to Jesus Christ and accept him as your Savior?

A. I do.

Q. Do you put your whole trust in his grace and love?

A. I do.

Q. Do you promise to follow and obey him as your Lord?

A. I do.

The Baptismal Covenant

Celebrant Will you continue in the apostles' teaching and fellowship, in the breaking of bread, and in the prayers?

People I will, with God's help.

Celebrant Will you persevere in resisting evil, and, whenever you fall into sin, repent and return to the Lord?

People I will, with God's help.

Celebrant Will you proclaim by word and example the Good News of God in Christ?

People I will, with God's help.

Celebrant Will you seek and serve Christ in all persons, loving your neighbor as yourself?

People I will, with God's help.

Celebrant Will you strive for justice and peace among all people, and respect the dignity of every human being?

People I will, with God's help.[10]

Thanksgiving over the Water

The Celebrant blesses the water, first saying The Lord be with you.

People And also with you.

Celebrant Let us give thanks to the Lord.

People It is right to give him thanks and praise.

Celebrant We thank you, Almighty God, for the gift of water. Over it the Holy Spirit moved in the beginning of creation. Through it you led the children of Israel out of their bondage in Egypt into the land of promise. In it your Son Jesus received the baptism of John and was anointed by the Holy Spirit as the Messiah, the Christ, to lead us, through his death and resurrection, from the bondage of sin into everlasting life.

We thank you, Father, for the water of Baptism. In it we are buried with Christ in his death. By it we share in his resurrection. Through it we are reborn by the Holy Spirit.

Therefore in joyful obedience to your Son, we bring into his fellowship those who come to him in faith, baptizing them in the Name of the Father, and of the Son, and of the Holy Spirit.

At the following words, the Celebrant touches the water

Now sanctify this water, we pray you, by the power of your Holy Spirit, that those who here are cleansed from sin and born again may continue for ever in the risen life of Jesus Christ our Savior.

To him, to you, and to the Holy Spirit, be all honor and glory, now and for ever. Amen.[11]

All this reeks of hospitality. How can the church possibly take responsibility for the ills that maim and destroy God's children? The task is overwhelming. It's hopeless, except that gestures of hospitality work magic. Whenever one of us is willing to make the caring, welcoming, or sharing gesture, others find the courage to join in.

Holy hospitality is the essence of the ministry that belongs to the Body of Christ. When we set aside the nonessentials, faithfulness is simply making sure that all God's creatures are fed, clothed, nurtured—in short—living the abundant life God promises.

The eucharist, then, is the ritual expression of the patterns of ministry that identify Christians in the world. It is only when we approach worship from this vantage point that we are able to keep before us the ministry to which we are called.

Worship as Justice

We are incarnational Christians. We believe that God is among us, and that in God's presence, we are working to realize God's Realm in our world and in our lives. If the work of Christ's Body in the world has to do with feeding and being fed, if it has to do with righting wrongs and healing brokenness, then the focus of catholic (universal) context on symbol and image makes perfect sense. Worship must be tactile. It is about sensing God's presence, not just thinking about it.

Worship, in a catholic (or if you will, eucharistic) context, is all about seeing, hearing, feeling, smelling, and tasting God's presence in God's world. All the senses are available to grasp the impact of the gospel—the teaching of Jesus—on the lives we live, day by day. What follows is framed around the assumption that the experience of worship engages all the senses.

The world of science fiction suggests that the evolution of the human animal is toward a state in which being is purely intellectual. Everyone has seen bad movies whose characters have rudimentary bodies barely able to support heads containing huge and powerful brains. As we imagine the evolution of Christian practice and theology from the early church, through the sixteenth-century Reformation, a movement toward a more cerebral expression of the faith is obvious. If one looks across the denominational (and nondenominational) landscape, one sees expressions of the faith ranging from truly incarnational (sacramental) to utterly cerebral (confessional) patterns. . . .

The work of establishing justice in the world is a daunting task. Faithful Christians are continually tempted to rationalize an escape from that charge. It is easy to articulate reasons for avoiding social responsibility, but when one is face to face with hunger, homelessness, or injustice, it is difficult not to respond.

Spirituality is a natural and essential part of human existence and thus is an important aspect of the life of the church. It is essential, however, that spiritual practice be balanced with a commitment to ministries of peace and justice in the world. Engaging the senses helps to create a balance between piety and ministry. As we taste, hear, smell, see, feel the world we inhabit and as we move around in it, we are reminded that we are creatures. When we engage the senses in worship—with incense, bread, wine, fabric, an embrace, music, and solemn procession—we are reminded that we are God's creatures and that we are called to live as one Body in God's creation.

And the daunting prospect of being Christ's Body in the world brings us back to the theme of hospitality. The beginning of the journey toward wholeness in creation is encounter with the other. When we put ourselves in the presence of need, our hearts melt, rationalization fails. And so the boundaries of our liturgical communities need to be permeable. It must be possible for all sorts and conditions of human life to gather around the table. When we "go . . . into the main streets, and invite everyone [we] find to the wedding banquet" (Matt. 22:9), the community re-creates itself in a new and transformative way. It becomes the wholeness it seeks to proclaim.

The Sunday morning worship experience is filled with opportunities to make gestures of welcome and hospitality. Those who serve as ushers and greeters, members of the altar guild, acolytes and eucharistic ministers, singers and instrumentalists, composers and poets are all in positions of high visibility. Their ministries on behalf of the congregation can signal either an atmosphere of exclusivity and control, or an attitude of welcome, inclusivity, and abundance.

7 ▪ Becoming the People of God

The liturgy is not a performance. The liturgy is an art form that is not meant to entertain or impress or edify or instruct. It is a corporate act of the people of God that aims to change us, to draw us out of our self-conscious preoccupations and deeper into the mystery of the dying and rising love of God for us and for this world. It is an encounter with God's own presence.

Granted, it is not always immediately clear that anything like this is happening in a typical church on a Sunday morning. Would a complete stranger to the Christian faith have any inkling of the vast mystery we gather to encounter here?

The author Annie Dillard suggests the answer is no:

> On the whole, I do not find Christians, outside of the catacombs, sufficiently sensible of conditions. Does anyone have the foggiest idea what sort of power we so blithely invoke? Or, as I suspect, does no one believe a word of it? The churches are children playing on the floor with their chemistry sets, mixing up a batch of TNT to kill a Sunday morning. It is madness to wear ladies' straw hats and velvet hats to church; we should all be wearing crash helmets. Ushers should issue life preservers and signal flares; they should lash us to our pews. For the sleeping god may wake someday and take offense, or the waking god may draw us out to where we can never return.[12]

Dillard shocks us with her strong words, but maybe we—like that sleeping god—need to wake up. Some say the worst and most persistent sin the church continues to commit is to bore people. It is worth pondering.

While the texts and verbal images used to address God may be attention-grabbing, we believe a much more powerful factor in the experience of a given act of worship may well be the whole complex of non-verbal gestures and actions that accompany the words, including the music being sung or heard. The building itself where worship is being conducted may be the most powerful factor of all. If the building in which you are worshiping looks and feels like a Gothic cathedral with altar, clergy, and choir at one far end of the building and the majority of people confined to fixed pews, that will be a very different experience than worshipping in a contemporary or renovated space with movable chairs that enable people and clergy to gather freely around an altar table in their midst.

There are many valid architectural options, just as there are many styles of music appropriate to worship, many forms of visual arts, a whole range of gestures, processions, even fragrances to enliven worship. None of these things is an end to itself. The key to making effective use of any or all of them lies in the intention and planning with which they are deployed and their purpose in supporting the whole point of a liturgical gathering.

If sacraments make visibly real what is already inwardly true, then the quality of the materials that make up the outward and visible sign matters very much. There is no doubt that God can use a tasteless, dry disk of wheat and flour to communicate the bread of heaven to God's people. Wouldn't the experience of that feeding be quite different if the material of the sacrament were a large, fragrant loaf baked by a member of the congregation, broken into fragments for everyone to share?

We have no misgivings that the baptism of a child accomplished by three drops of water passing through three inches of air absolutely incorporates that child into the Body of Christ. It will be a very different human experience if that baptism bathes the child or adult in plenty of water, maybe running water, enough to splash around in and even potentially dangerous. How better to make the point that this bath is a participation in the passing over of Christ from death to new life?

We long to see the perfumed oil used to anoint the newly baptized poured and massaged lovingly onto their foreheads as they are signed with the cross. A respected priest and teacher in the Episcopal Church, John Westerhoff, once said impishly: "We can continue to talk all we want to about baptism as a participation in the death and resurrection of Jesus, but no one ever drowned from being dribbled on."

What if all the members of our congregations engaged regularly in brief and inviting rehearsals so that everyone might join with gusto in the singing of new music? What if congregations were invited and taught to participate fully in the liturgy, not just in the spoken recitation of group texts, but in the full range of the "choreography" that belongs to them: bowing and kneeling and processing and making the sign of the cross and unashamedly raising their hands in prayer as their ancestors in the faith did?

We set a lavish welcome table because our mission is to meet the desperate hungers of the world. We welcome, wash, and anoint new members because our mission is to wash and tend the wounds of those who have no help or hope. We praise God together because God is simply God, the creator, the sustainer, the possibility of life itself. We are made in God's image and made for community, and our mission is to proclaim the goodness of God to a world that believes it has created and sustains itself and is therefore free to do to creation whatever it likes. We need to know what these things feel like. We need to practice them to be effective agents of God's mission of restoring all things to right relationship.

It is important to remember that God doesn't need liturgy. We do. In the Book of Common Prayer's form for the liturgy of Ash Wednesday, after a lengthy confession of sin, the bishop or priest assures the people of God's forgiveness and then says, "Therefore we beseech him to grant us true repentance and his Holy Spirit, that those things may please him which we do on this day . . . so that at the last we may come to his eternal joy; through Jesus Christ our Lord."[13] We naturally want to please God with our prayer, but we are not performing a pageant or a play so that God will notice and delight in us.

The Christian life does involve change and growth, some of it painful. In fact following Jesus leads us inexorably to the cross. So praying with a fierce tenderness, celebrating the sacraments with conviction, and making lavish use of the good things of creation—water, oil, bread, wine, reverent human touch, the power of communal song—we need these things, not just to be "good" Christian people, but to be fully human beings. In the society in which many of us live now, connected electronically but increasingly isolated from face-to-face community, reckoning with social and economic shock and global climate change, we need the human arts of gathering. We need rituals that commit us to something greater than ourselves, that speak to us of our utter reliance on the power of God working in and through us. We need these things to equip us to take up the cross and to find the only real life worth living.

Notes

1 Robert Taft, "What Does Liturgy Do? Toward a Soteriology of Liturgical Celebration: Some Theses," in *Primary Sources of Liturgical Theology*, ed. Dwight Vogel (Collegeville, MN: Liturgical Press, 2000), 139.

2 Augustine, "Sermon 272," in *The Works of St. Augustine*, Vol. III/7, trans. Edmund Hill (New Rochelle: New City Press, 1993), 300–301.

3 Taft, "What Does Liturgy Do?," 143–44.

4 Jeffrey D. Lee, *Opening the Prayer Book*, vol. 7 of *The New Church's Teaching Series* (Cambridge, MA: Cowley Publications, 1999), 159.

5 Phoebe Pettingell, "Introduction," *Enriching Our Worship 1: Morning and Evening Prayer, The Great Litany, The Holy Eucharist* (New York: Church Publishing, 1998), 8.

6 Resolution A068, the 79th General Convention of the Episcopal Church, Austin, Texas, July 2018.

7 Jennifer M. Phillips, "Praying Rightly: The Poetics of Liturgy," in *Gleanings: Essays on Expansive Language with Prayers for Various Occasions*, ed. Ruth A. Meyers and Phoebe Pettingell (New York: Church Publishing, 2001), 11.

8 Lee, *Opening the Prayer Book*, 154–55.

9 The Book of Common Prayer, 855–56.

10 The Book of Common Prayer. 302–5.

11 The Book of Common Prayer, 306–7.

12 Annie Dillard, *Teaching a Stone to Talk: Expeditions and Encounter* (New York: Harper & Row, 1982), 40–41.

13 The Book of Common Prayer, 269.

TURN: Pause, listen, and choose to follow Jesus

THE WAY OF LOVE

*As Jesus was walking along, he saw Levi son of
   Alphaeus sitting at the tax booth, and he said to
   him, "Follow me." And he got up and followed him.
   – Mark 2:14*

*"Do you turn to Jesus Christ . . . ?"
   – Book of Common Prayer, 302*

Like the disciples, we are called by Jesus to follow the Way
of Love. With God's help, we can turn from the powers of
sin, hatred, fear, injustice, and oppression toward the
way of truth, love, hope, justice, and freedom. In turning,
we reorient our lives to Jesus Christ, falling in love again, again, and again.

For Reflection and Discernment

- What practices help you to turn again and again to Jesus and the Way of Love?
- How will (or do) you incorporate these practices into your rhythm of life?
- Who will be your companion as you turn toward Jesus?

LEARN: Reflect on Scripture each day, especially on Jesus's life and teachings.

*"Those who love me will keep my word, and my Father will love them,
   and we will come to them and make our home with them." – John 14:23*

*Grant us so to hear [the Holy Scriptures], read, mark, learn, and inwardly
   digest them. – Book of Common Prayer, 236*

By reading and reflecting on Scripture, especially the life and teachings of
Jesus, we draw near to God, and God's word dwells in us. When we open our
minds and hearts to Scripture, we learn to see God's story and God's activity
in everyday life.

For Reflection and Discernment

- What ways of reflecting on Scripture are most life-giving for you?
- When will you set aside time to read and reflect on Scripture in your day?
- With whom will you share in the commitment to read and reflect on Scripture?

PRAY: Dwell intentionally with God daily

He was praying in a certain place, and after he had finished,
  one of his disciples said to him, "Lord, teach us to pray,
  as John taught his disciples." – Luke 11:1

"Lord, hear our prayer." – Book of Common Prayer

Jesus teaches us to come before God with humble hearts, boldly offering our thanksgivings and concerns to God or simply listening for God's voice in our lives and in the world. Whether in thought, word, or deed, individually or corporately, when we pray we invite and dwell in God's loving presence.

For Reflection and Discernment

- What intentional prayer practices center you in God's presence, so you can hear, speak, or simply dwell with God?
- How will (or do) you incorporate intentional prayer into your daily life?
- With whom will you share in the commitment to pray?

WORSHIP: Gather in community weekly to thank, praise, and dwell with God

When he was at the table with them, he took bread, blessed and broke it,
  and gave it to them. Then their eyes were opened, and they recognized him.
  – Luke 24:30-31

Celebrant: Lift up your hearts. People: We lift them to the Lord.
  – Book of Common Prayer, 361

When we worship, we gather with others before God. We hear the Good News of Jesus, give thanks, confess, and offer the brokenness of the world to God. As we break bread, our eyes are opened to the presence of Christ. By the power of the Holy Spirit, we are made one body, the body of Christ sent forth to live the Way of Love.

For Discernment and Reflection

- What communal worship practices move you to encounter God and knit you into the body of Christ?
- How will (or do) you commit to regularly worship?
- With whom will you share the commitment to worship this week?

BLESS: Share faith and unselfishly give and serve

"Freely you have received; freely give." – Matthew 10:8

Celebrant: Will you proclaim by word and example the Good News of God in Christ?
People: We will, with God's help. – Book of Common Prayer, 305

Jesus called his disciples to give, forgive, teach, and heal in his name. We are empowered by the Spirit to bless everyone we meet, practicing generosity and compassion and proclaiming the Good News of God in Christ with hopeful words and selfless actions. We can share our stories of blessing and invite others to the Way of Love.

For Discernment and Reflection

- What are the ways the Spirit is calling you to bless others?
- How will (or does) blessing others through sharing your resources, faith, and story become part of your daily life?
- Who will join you in committing to the practice of blessing others

GO: Cross boundaries, listen deeply, and live like Jesus

Jesus said to them, "Peace be with you. As the Father has sent me,
so I send you." – John 20:21

Send them into the world in witness to your love.
– Book of Common Prayer, 306

As Jesus went to the highways and byways, he sends us beyond our circles and comfort to witness to the love, justice, and truth of God with our lips and with our lives. We go to listen with humility and to join God in healing a hurting world. We go to become Beloved Community, a people reconciled in love with God and one another.

For Discernment and Reflection

- To what new places or communities is the Spirit sending you to witness to the love, justice, and truth of God?
- How will you build into your life a commitment to cross boundaries, listen carefully, and take part in healing and reconciling what is broken in this world?
- With whom will you share in the commitment to go forth as a reconciler and healer?

REST: Receive the gift of God's grace, peace, and restoration

Peace I leave with you; my peace I give you. I do not give to you
as the world gives. Do not let your hearts be troubled
and do not be afraid. – John 14:27

Blessed are you, O Lord . . . giving rest to the weary,
renewing the strength of those who are spent.
– Book of Common Prayer, 113

From the beginning of creation, god has established the sacred pattern of going and returning, labor and rest. Especially today, God invites us to dedicate time for restoration and wholeness—within our bodies, minds, and souls, and within our communities and institutions. By resting, we place our trust in God; the primary actor who brings all things to their fullness.

For Discernment and Reflection

- What practices restore your body, mind and soul?
- How will you observe rest and renewal on a regular basis?
- With whom will you commit to create and maintain a regular practice of rest?